Yukon Ho!

A Calvin and Hobbes Collection
by Bill Watterson

Andrews McMeel
Publishing, LLC

Kansas City • Sydney • London

ISBN-13: 978-1-4494-0708-7

www.andrewsmcmeel.com

The Yukon Song

My tiger friend has got the sled,
And I have packed a snack.
We're all set for the trip ahead.
We're never coming back!

We're abandoning this life we've led!
So long, Mom and Pop!
We're sick of doing what you've said,
And now it's going to stop!

We're going where it snows all year,
Where life can have real meaning.
A place where we won't have to hear,
"Your room could stand some cleaning."

The Yukon is the place for us!
That's where we want to live.
Up there we'll get to yell and cuss,
And act real primitive.

We'll never have to go to school,
Forced into submission,
By monstrous, crabby teachers who'll
Make us learn addition.

We'll never have to clean a plate,
Of veggie glops and goos.
Messily we'll masticate,
Using any fork we choose!

The timber wolves will be our friends.
We'll stay up late and howl,
At the moon, till nighttime ends,
Before going on the prowl.

Oh, what a life! We cannot wait,
To be in that arctic land,
Where we'll be masters of our fate,
And lead a life that's grand!

No more of parental rules!
We're heading for some snow!
Good riddance to those grown-up ghouls!
We're leaving! *Yukon Ho!*

I'M HOME!

8

9

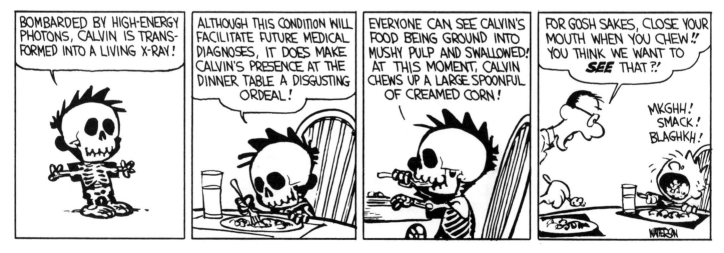

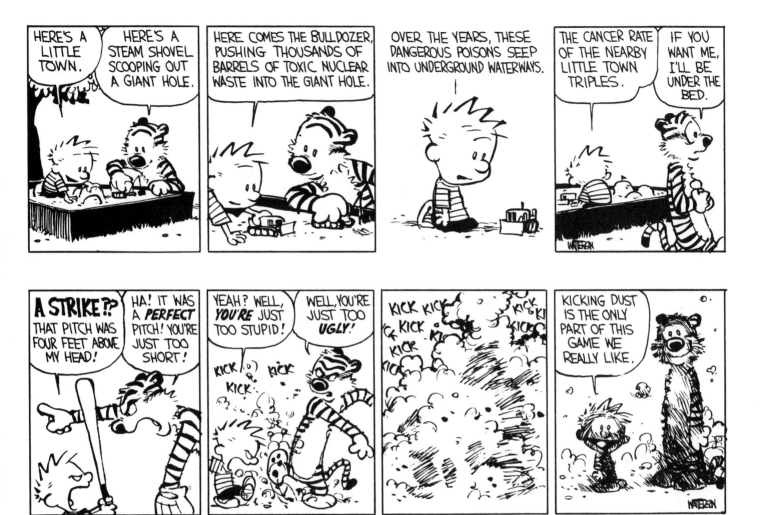

13

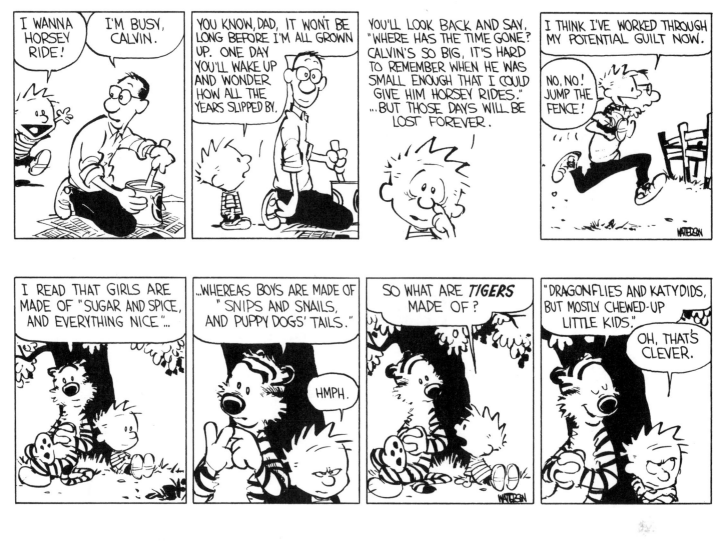

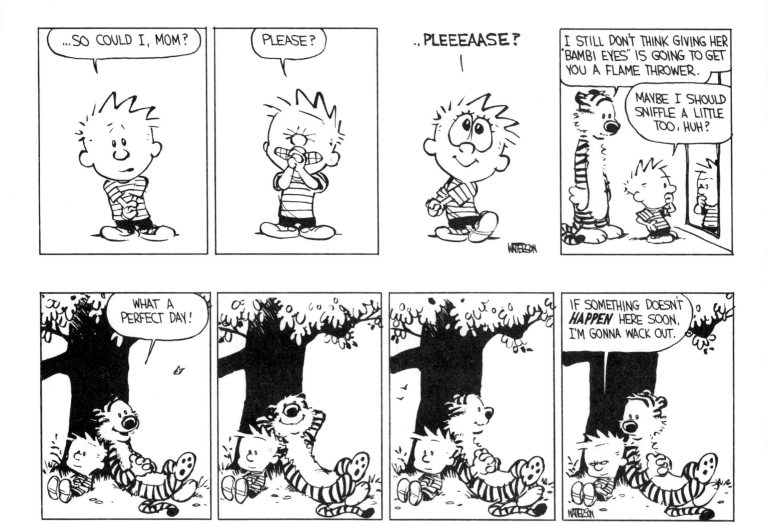

26

37

42

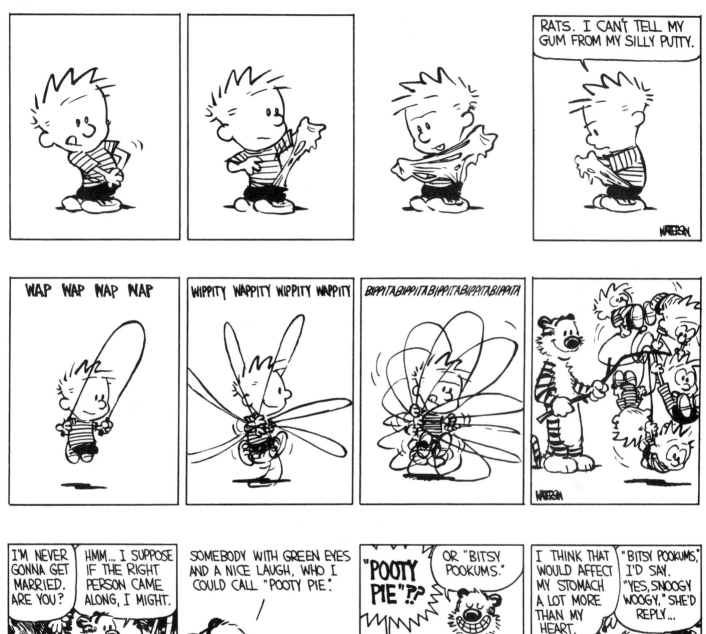

58

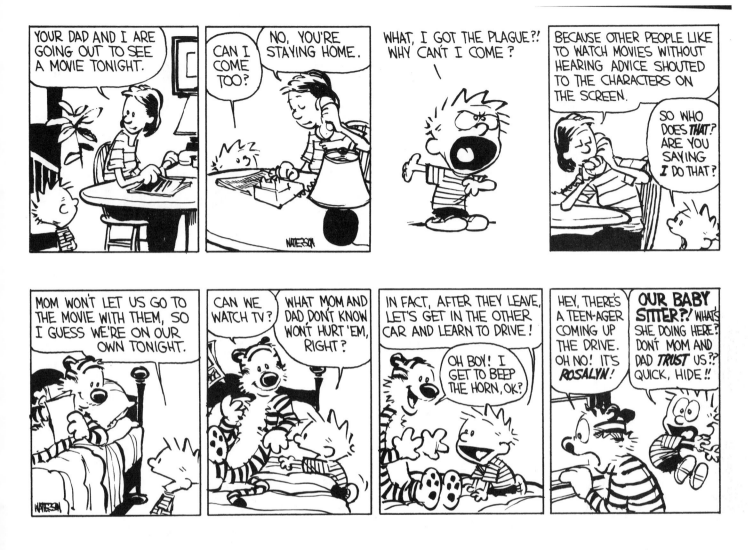

66

73

SNIP SNAP CRACK

SHICKA SHICKA WHISSSHH

F SHOOF SHOOF SHOOF SHO

KRITCH KRUNCH KRITCH KRUNCH

SOMETIMES IT'S GOOD TO HUSH UP AWHILE AND LET AUTUMN STICK IN A FEW WORDS.

PROCESSED LUNCH MEAT IS PRETTY SCARY. WHAT **ARE** THESE LITTLE SPECKS, ANYWAY? LIZARD PARTS? WHO KNOWS?

AND THIS "SKIN": I HEARD IT USED TO BE MADE OF INTESTINE, BUT I THINK NOWADAYS IT'S PLASTIC.

OF COURSE, THEY DYE AND WAX FRUIT SO IT LOOKS BETTER. IT'S LIKE EATING A CANDLE.

AND MOM WONDERS WHY I'M SO HUNGRY AFTER SCHOOL.

YEP, WE'D PROBABLY BE DEAD NOW IF IT WASN'T FOR TWINKIES.

BON VOYAGE DAD

75

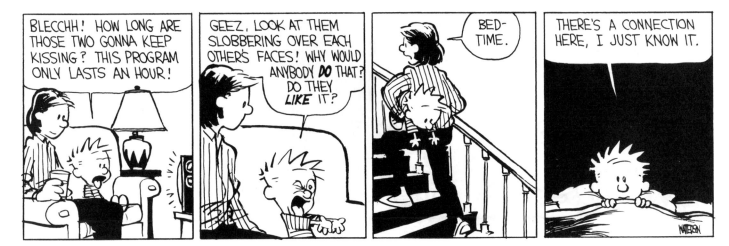

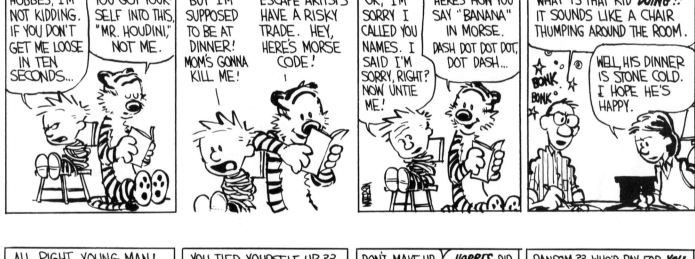

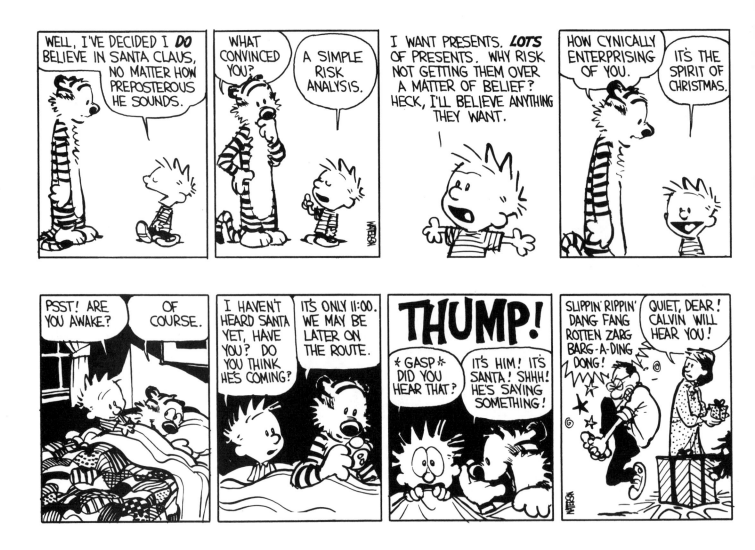

114

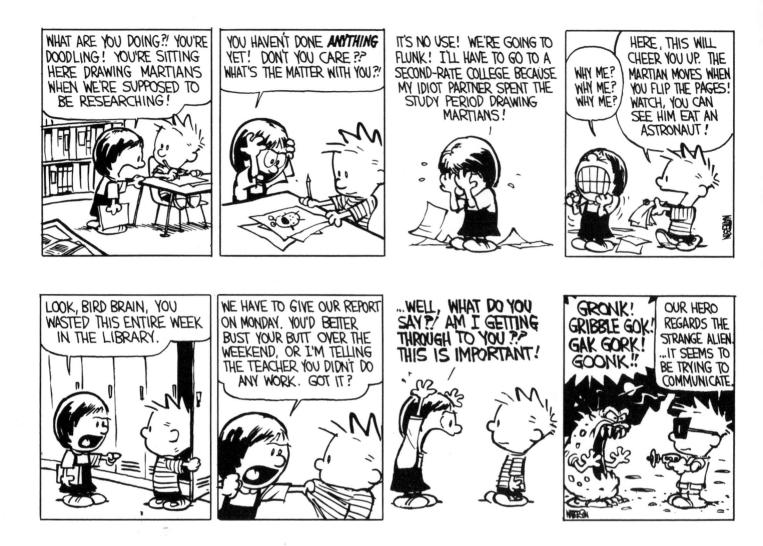

125

The End